CLASS WAR

PUNCH

in the Schoolroom

Edited by William Hewison

A PUNCH BOOK

Published in association with

GRAFTON BOOKS

A Division of the Collins Publishing Group

Grafton Books
A Division of the Collins Publishing Group
8 Grafton Street, London W1X 3LA

Published by Grafton Books 1988

British Library Cataloguing in Publication Data

Class war: Punch in the schoolroom.
1. English humorous cartoons – Collections
I. Hewison, Bill
741.5'942

ISBN 0-246-13399-6

Printed in Great Britain by William Collins Sons & Co. Ltd, Glasgow

Introduction

Every class has its clown. In my time it was Tommy Scrafton, a sharp-nosed lad who had raised teacher-baiting to a sublime level that combined high art with low cunning. In one memorable skirmish the maths master, stoked up by Scrafton to near apoplexy, spat a full set of dentures across the front row of desks. Scrafton, with a disguised attempt at a slip catch, managed to punch them out through the window. The rest of us, of course, rolled in the aisles.

The professional humorist, however, can't rely on wayward opportunities like that; he has to sit down and sweat at the business, kick-start the cogs of his inventiveness into some sort of movement and hope that his toiling will be rewarded with one or two comical ideas. The cartoonist operates in the same way but he also has to be able to draw the ideas once he has kneaded them into shape. It's no use producing an idea concerning, say, the Charge of the Light Brigade, if drawing it is beyond his knowledge and ability. Better stick to the familiar, everyday scene where that kind of problem does not arise.

Schooldays are familiar. Cartoonists, like the rest of us, have gone through the educational mill so they have plenty of experience to draw on but, curiously, most of them seldom do. What really interests them and what provides the basic material for their ideas most of the time is what's happening in the classroom *now* – the various topical shifts and changes they read about in the newspapers and see on the Nine O'Clock News. So their offerings in *Punch*, for instance, are a sort of social history, but one bent through the distorting prism of humorous comment, some of it benign, some of it critical. The use of pocket calculators and the arrival of language labs, co-ed schools, classroom violence, lefty teachers, sex education – as these appear on the scene our artist jokesmiths give them the full treatment.

The few cartoonists who also scrutinise the fundamental, day-to-day functioning of the school – the subject lessons, school reports, homework, sports days, examinations, Parents' Days, and so on – are usually those cartoonists who have doubled up as teachers at one time or another. There aren't that many of them but their stuff has a particular glow of authenticity about it, as you will readily recognise in the following pages. Look out for the signatures of J.W. Taylor, Dickinson, Bill Stott and Larry – each of these comic artists has served his time up at the sharp end and their pens probe areas the others seldom reach. However, cartoonists have families, too, and their kids bring back dispatches from that same battle-front, so all in all not much is missed. There are the "regular" subjects, of course, those which are near clichés like the Careers master dishing out advice (or not), and school buses, and lollipop crossings; I have included a select sprinkling.

As for the depiction of the *dramatis personae*, these *Punch* humorists have relied on a pictorial shorthand where, keeping pace with change, the gowned and mortar-boarded schoolmaster gave way to the tweedy pipe smoker with leather elbow patches, who in turn evolved into the bearded sociologist with an axe to grind. Exaggerations, certainly, but recognisable.

So here, then, is a risible account of a trek through the blackboard jungle, one which Tommy Scrafton, his schooldays long behind him, would surely approve.

William Hewison
March 1988

"I really wanted to go to Cambridge."

"If I've got to teach it, headmaster, I'll teach it in my own way and nobody else's."

*"I tell you, Jackson, I wish I'd listened to **my** careers master."*

"Sir, school uniforms stifle individuality…"

*"Here at St Jude's we specialise in
the gifted vandal."*

*"In **our** class's Christmas pageant,
I'm playing the
department store manager."*

"Turn her round and head for the amusement arcade."

"'Ere, sir – how come our disruptive
action is bad but your disruptive action
in support of a pay claim is OK?"

"Parents' Day is tomorrow, Mrs. Jackson."

"Now, sir, you say the vandals got in last night and wrecked the classrooms but no one noticed until about 11.45 this morning."

"Of course, overcrowding is our biggest problem."

"Solicitors can make a lot of money. Yes, if I were you I'd mug a solicitor."

*"Oh, the alphabet, and
programming our microcomputer."*

"Is there anyone at all on the shop floor who can give these youngsters Work Experience?"

"I will now explain the progressive methods by which your children are taught – so keep quiet, sit up straight and don't fidget."

"Well, another day – another learning experience."

"Yes, but famous at what?"

"If it's sex, I'd better stay up and watch it – we're bound to be asked a question about it at school tomorrow."

"Frankly, Mr and Mrs Rumbelow, I'm a little worried about
your William – I don't know who the hell he is!"

"And even after your three years'
student's grant, there'll be your social
security benefits to bank."

OUR FOUNDER

DEPT. OF
EVOLUTIONARY
BIOLOGY

SCHWADRon

JUDE'S
PRIMARY
SCHOOL

Dickinson

*"Next year we can smash the
comprehensive, then if we work hard
there's university…"*

"I'm glad we changed over to mixed ability groups – you always get a fair proportion who couldn't punch their way out of a paper bag."

*"You shout 'eureka' just **once** more."*

"Please, sir, I'd like to be a barber."

"I see here that you were school bully for three years."

"This is old Chalkey Chumley's motor. It must be for sale."

"Right, girls – round the room once, hand Miss Rogers your cheque, then on to the next class."

"We were relieved to find a school that wasn't soft on uniforms."

*"You know as well as I do, Mrs Watson,
that Kevin's whole appearance is cocking a snook
at authority."*

"To delegate? Ask your mother, son!"

"Stop bothering your Dad, Lenny. You're old enough now
to go and belt the Housemaster one yourself."

"My father says if he'd
had sex education
at school he wouldn't
be worrying about
mine now."

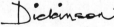

THE AMOEBA

"At what stage does the amoeba
say to itself – 'I'm going to tell
my dad if you don't stop'?"

"I've been expelled for
coming top in sex education."

"My dad says you taught him sex
when you were at primary
school together."

"Right – where's the Cow Gum Monitor?"

"Blimey – is that before or after?"

"Today, we begin the 'going down with our ship' course."

"That's the trouble with playschool – they just train them to make a collage out of everything…"

$$A = \frac{x}{y}(14 \cdot 7\pi) + \sqrt[4]{\sqrt{3}}(2r)$$
$$B \simeq x(n-1) \therefore a + \left(\frac{\pi}{2}\right) - \frac{1}{3}r$$
$$\therefore B + A \cos x$$
$$= \sqrt{r+1} \, \tan r$$

"Professor Ziegler's working on a way to get our research grant renewed."

"Halt – who goes there?"

ARMY CATERING SCHOOL

Kreme Porrige Betta
Beatle Kleen Kumfy
BisKit Chilprufe
Glo Weetflakes
Krisp
Juce Kolefyre

Hollowood

*"We mustn't sneer at commerce,
children: it's just that in Spelling it
has rather different standards."*

"You're lucky to be able to use your degree, man."

*"Bridget is to be the ovum in the school
fertilisation play."*

"The sky is falling! The sky is falling!"

"Your complete ignorance on every other subject is only matched by your detailed knowledge of each provision on corporal punishment by the European Court of Human Rights."

"Write an essay on – yes, yes, Warburton,
you can give out the aerosols."

*"It's a father's **right** to help his son."*

*"Look! There it is – **that's** his peg."*

"Dropping out? Good! We're incorporating dropping out in our new Faculty of De-structured Combined Social Studies."

"Shall we put down 'some form of community service', Bowker?"

LERNHAM GRAMMAR SCHOOL
PARENTS' DAY

*"I meant the **boys'** parents, Melton!"*

"Who's in charge of Nature Table?"

"Ho, that's Madcap Meg of the Upper Fourth."

"As I understand it, we progress through play spaces and adventure playgrounds to leisure centres."

"Very well, Geoffrey – you have received fair warning. I am going to confiscate your brick."

*"Cuts, cuts, cuts – where will it all
end, Miss Benson?"*

*"You'd do far better to find yourself
a public school type, Joanna – I had
all my sex repressions steamed out of
me at a comprehensive school."*

"There's growing concern at the increasing political content of your cookery lessons."

"And this is Jenkins, our faithful old teaching aids maintenance engineer."

"It might be freedom in space to him, but to me it will always be 12 metres of chicken wire, 75 litres of Polycell, 102 Daily Expresses, 51 Observers and 7 Exchange & Marts."

*"Now, Shirley – you can't be a blasted oak **every** time."*

"Look – if you have five pocket calculators and I take two
away, how many have you got left?"

"Little devils – they know very well it should be your maths period."

"Ethnic Pride Day is tomorrow, Arthur."

"The State University, ever mindful of the contributions of all
citizens to the community
would, on this occasion, like to confer on you
the honorary degree of Doctor of Leisure."

*"Oh, the new teacher's all right. He's congenial, eager
to please and responsive to suggestions."*

"Got five hundred lines to do, Mum – how d'you spell 'promiscuous'!"

"Could you spare Lust, Sloth and Pollution for a run through Act Two?"

"*The new boy from Stratford, I suspect.*"

"*I think the ox wants a wee.*"

H.M.PRISON
MODERN
ART
CLASS

"Stockbroking's a good career. Yes, if
I were you I'd marry a stockbroker."

"The way you teach 'otpot, it's no wonder
our Sandra's marriage is on the rocks."

"He used to whistle all day before he started
on his adult literacy course."

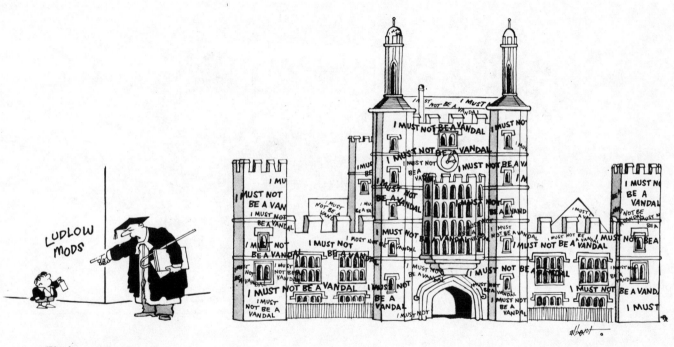

*"You boy, write out sixty times
'I must not be a vandal.'"*

*"Actually, I'm busy with a tutorial – Geoffrey's hearing my
essay on Some Suggestions for the Organisation and Administration of
University Education."*

*"Yesterday? … The music course finished **yesterday**?"*

"She must be halfway through her adult literacy course."

"To be quite frank, I'm not sure whether form captains are authorised to perform marriages."

"I suppose you thought we dons spent all our time writing detective novels and inventing crossword puzzles."

*"I wonder if Car Maintenance would have been
Charlotte Brontë's second choice?"*

*"I often say, Mrs Dent, I'd rather have your little Christopher in my class than **all** the bright, clever ones!"*

"I have a question — would you agree that the most vital art produced in the novel is when the novelist is emancipated from the closed morality of conventional beliefs, while not losing his sense of concrete actuality?"

"If the worst comes to the worst he can always go into his father's business, of course."

"Can I take an apple for the co-ordinator of interdisciplinary studies in the environmental faculty?"

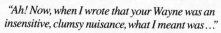

"Ah! Now, when I wrote that your Wayne was an insensitive, clumsy nuisance, what I meant was…"

"We're going to have to confiscate your tuckbox, Smith!"

*"You mean to say you are Mr Grimshaw and little Gavin **doesn't** live in a fantasy world?"*

"Boys, this is Constable Wilkins, who's here
to deliver a lot of sentimental twaddle
about crossing the road safely."

"Actually, sir, I was rather relying on nepotism. Jones Minor is going to ask his dad to get me a union card for a job in my pater's factory!"

*"Gone are the days when a double first led straight
to a plum job in Whitehall."*

"When did you last see the father?"

"Would the gifted children carry on quietly with the chapter on Propositional Calculus."

"You say there are some university students waiting for me?"

"Don't tell me! It's Mrs Mason – I'd recognise Jason's project anywhere."

"The Asian boys keep vanishing."

"Quelch has had a stroke. Bunter has received a postal-order and Bob Cherry is a card-carrying member of the NUJ. It's the end of Greyfriars as we know it."

"Oh, by the way...according to my teacher I'm suffering from a lack
of discipline in the home. See to it, will you...?"

"These mock GCE results are awful.
Heaven knows what your father is
going to pretend to do to you!"

"There's this about my old school – that careers master certainly knew his stuff!"

"Dig that! Through to max revs in three seconds."

"*Your work, Charlesworth, has improved enormously. And now that you've cut down on smoking, all that remains is for you to get the boozing licked.*"

"*An admirable attempt to drag Handicraft out of the Dark Ages, but if the P.T.A. gets wind of it, you're up the spout.*"

"*Of* **course** *it's better to be an unemployed graduate than an unemployed petrol pump attendant!*"

"If you don't improve your sums, dear, you're going to be stymied when you have to start counting calories."

"…but in my heart I'm a C cup."

"We'll come to the design of steeple fund boards later in the course, Millgrove."

"You'll find Eton a mixed-ability school, too, Hobson. It's produced twenty British Prime Ministers of varying degrees of competence."

"H.M. Schools Inspector! Switch to discussing how the national economic cake is divided up."

"The shortage of paper is getting serious!"

"I see the cuts are beginning to take effect."

"It's not quite what I imagined from the prospectus."

"He's anchor man in the inter-house relay."

"Good Heavens, Adkins! Didn't they teach you **anything** at the
Harvard Business School?"

"*In sex education class, they're teaching the girls how to use sex as a weapon.*"

"You a school teacher?"

"I'm setting a timed essay on why your own faculty should not be axed, using both sides of the paper."

"They've told me to stand outside until they feel like behaving themselves."

"And how are our new infants behaving this morning?"

"*And I'd like to thank Colonel Hetherington for his contribution to the nature table.*"

"My ambitions are slightly less than yours – I
just want the class I teach to disarm."

"…and lastly, congratulations on graduating
before the price-tag hit sixty thou!"

"Quite frankly, I don't think the sun god's going to give a damn about your sociology degree."

*"Sex Instruction: Satisfactory. Steady
prurience."*

"…And then came the war."

"Not sex again!"

"I got my degree and was looking forward to a nice, long period of idle disenchantment, when what happens? I'm offered a job!"

"Need I remind you, gentlemen, that we're here to study anatomy?"

"It's an exclusive little Comprehensive for
the children of Shadow Ministers."

"We were shattered to learn he was dyslectic.
We thought he was learning Bulgarian."

"Bloody student drop-outs!"

"Anyway, to get back to this rat we were dissecting."

"Start as you mean to go on, that's what I say!"

"Very impressive, Ainsworth – but I have
no information on how one becomes a
bouncer."

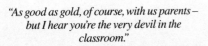

"As good as gold, of course, with us parents –
but I hear you're the very devil in the
classroom."

*"Remember Tom Gribble, tall dark lad, with us in 2B, always top of
the form, good athlete, everybody liked him…?"*